UNIVERSAL HANDBOOK

First Essential Steps into the Universe

OLGA KHARITONOVA

BALBOA.
PRESS
A DIVISION OF HAY HOUSE

Balboa Press books may be ordered through booksellers or by contacting:

Balboa Press
A Division of Hay House
1663 Liberty Drive
Bloomington, IN 47403
www.balboapress.com
1 (877) 407-4847

Print information available on the last page.

ISBN: 978-1-5043-8959-4 (sc)
ISBN: 978-1-5043-8960-0 (e)

Balboa Press rev. date: 09/30/2017

For all of us, who are moving Forward.
For that Magic Flying Now.
For the Change.
For All That Is.

FOREWORD

What this book is about.

I have heard several times, that reading several books at the same time is not a good idea.

The common opinión is that in this case our attention is not focused and we are not absorbing the information at the same level, as if it was one book at a time.

In my opinión its only a part of the truth in here.

Indeed, when we are totally focused on one subject, our concentration is higher, than in case of multifocusing. But everything is very individual and my visión is that human brain is an amazing mechanism, which can (and should) be used much more intensively,than its normally used now.

But in this chapter i would like to go a bit further and to talk about the importance of having a larger picture.

If we stick to one author and therefore – to the one conception and perception of the reality, then we limit ourselves and we risk not to get the whole and complete picture.

When i started to read spiritual books, I, being used to the popular concept ¨one book at a time¨, was reading profoundly one book and if i liked the author, i was buying her/his other books. And even though i was totally enjoying my reading, somewhere, on the background of my mind i had a feeling, that its only a part of the larger picture.

There are many great and exeptional authours in the self-help and spiritual field (Joe Dispenza, Denise Linn,Bruce Lipton, Brian Weiss and of course ¨the woman who started at all¨ - Louise Hay) and most of them are published under HAY HOUSE publishing house.

And there are other specialists in the spiritual field – highly professional as well (Robert Schwartz, Trutz Hardo, Dr. Stelzl etc.), whose work and books is definitely a sort of revelation for many readers. For those who are READY. For others that would be just fairy tales.

I sincerely admire people, who have the courage to reveal publicly things, which, from the one hand are open to everyone, but from the other- are contradictory to the common current model of living and sometimes (most of the times) just scary people.

Robert Schwartz, for example through his work, reveals us, that suicides, incests, miscarriages etc. are pre-born choices and not everybody is ready for this kind of information.

For me,for myself its clear, that if i would be only reading the authours, who´s focus lays on one perspective, I would not have the idea of the varios aspects of the Universe. I would not have a larger picture.

While some of us are fascinated by the great and profound Joe Dispenzas,Bruce Lipton´s etc. researches, the others deny science and respect and trust spiritual approach only. And what if all these seemingly different themes perfectly coexist and work together? Or even add each other? And give us indeed a larger picture.

What i see by my own expierence, is that most people have in their heads crazy spiritual or non-spiritual mix. Or they completely deny all "that spirituality" and stick only to scientifically proven ways of seeing the world, so these people are " too grounded". While the others are not grounded at all.

According to my observations, not so many people successfully combine spiritual way of living with grounded approach to the physical reality they live in.

Many people are still simply afraid or feel uncomfortable with the word "spiritual"(normally in the countries and places with strong church influence). What they dont understand or dont know, thats its impossible not to be spiritual, because You ARE Spirit.

Or we can see another extreme.

When spiritual people become so "spiritual", that they tend to be forget, that they are still in the physical form. These people, for instance, can refuse professional western medical help or can miss important appointments, because that morning they did not have time to meditate.

I start every morning with meditation. But every morning is not always the same one and sometimes i have an hour for meditation and sometimes only ten minutes. Im grateful for having time in both options and i chose one or another according to my plans.

My "spirituality" does not affect my agenda and therefore – the agenda of the people around me. Because living in the society we have some commitments and agreements with others.

I consider myself as a "spiritual" person and i start my day with my spiritual rituals, but my self-discipline is not a corset, which can not be open and my point here is that some "spiritual people"(or who consider themselves as "spiritual" ones) lack grounded flexibility.

We all – or almost all of us – have spiritual figure/ leader we admire and take an example from.

Many of us are inspired by Jesus, Mother Mary, Mother Theresa, Ghandi and other great Teachers. And they can really lead Your life to the better one.

But – from the other hand – we forget sometimes,that our life path/life plan is different from theirs. And our life conditions and life circumstances are different as well. And we can be infintelly inspired by our "favourite" spiritual figure, who probably lived thousands years ago, but WE live Here and Now and Life is always moving forward.

Yes, some things remain the same ("dont kill", " dont steal" etc.), but some are evolving according to the expansión of the Universe (and Universe is constantly expanding).

For example.

During the centuries people were supposed never divorce and live the whole life with the same person. And because of that so many people were unhappy. Times changed. And "rules" changed or are changing as well. So now we can enjoy several relationships during the one life time, because step by step we are taking our power and independence back.

We also start to realise, that no one is a property of anybody. And if for someone to spend the entire life with the same person is the ultimate life priority, that only means that this life visión is right for that particular person. So for another one this very same life model can (and noramlly does) lead to the feeling of deap unhappiness in case of failed marriage or broken relationship.

We – ALL of us – have individual and unique life plan and only WE, in the core of our being, can feel whats right exactly for us.

And what was right for Mother Theresa in Calcutta decades ago,probably (and likely is) is not right for some of us NOW.

Life is changing and moving forward every single second and we have to adapt to the current reality. We have to adapt to NOW. Thats, by my observations, is a problem for many "spiritual" people.

Some of them are still living according to the books, who someone have written and rewritten and rewritten (and many,many "re") 2,3,5 thousands of years ago.

Yes, there are eternal values, which are timless, but still. We always have to live our OWN life, according to OUR own life plan, OUR circumstances and according to OUR NOW.

Here i also see the Key, why authentic spirituality is still not considered seriously by "normal" people.

Its because what these "normal" people see is not adapted to the current reality. And there are still many "gurus" in weird outfits, who declare, that "to achieve an enlightment" one has to travel to India or Tibet.

Its nothing bad with travelling. In fact, its great and interesting and it enriches You in so many levels. Every trip and every new destination "expands" You and therefore _

Your energy field. New places and new people ARE new energies and information.

But there is NO trips that could ¨open¨ Your inner wisdoms and Keys, if they are simply not there.

Booking a flight to India does not automatically means, that You will come back a different person. You ¨could¨.

But ¨could¨ does not mean ¨will¨.

This kind of ¨guru´s communities¨ in most of the cases dont reflect and dont transmit authentic spirituality. And authentic spirituality is FREEDOM. Freedom from any ¨guru¨ and the way of living according to the one´s own Truth and wisdom. And this freedom is Everywhere. And everyone already holds this freedom within.

Within.

Not in Himalayas.

Everything is inside YOU and exactly where You are RIGHT NOW. And this NOW – this Magic Flying Now – has huge variety of aspects.

¨NOW¨ consists not only of the science, not only of the meditations. Its not only past life issues, its not only information from different adivination tools and its not only pre- birth planning.

Its EVERYTHING.

And only if You ¨study¨ this ¨everything¨, You - step by step – will be approaching to the understanding of the larger picture and how Universe really ¨functions¨.

I give You an example.

Lets imagine that You wish to be an owner of the red Ferrari or simply being rich. And being heard about the Law of Manifestation, You start to meditate to manifest the red Ferrari or a lot of money. Indeed, after some ammount of time and focused meditations You CAN ¨manifest¨ or ¨attract¨ that red Ferrari or a lot of money into Your life.

BUT.

If in Your pre-birth life plan is not indicated to be rich due to Your karmic debts or Your own personal pre-birth life choice (You could have chosen a financially modest life to feel/learn on contrast with previous wealthy lives), so this manifested money – first: will not make You happy(things, which are not in accordance with our life plan dont make us happy and by doing so, indicate us that we are going to the worng direction) and second : will be gone fast. Or You lose them or someone will steal them or You will just spend everything very quickly.

The same will happen with red Ferrari. You (or Your children/friends) can have an accident, in which Your car will be seriously damaged or it can be stolen.

So in fact – according to the Law of Free Will You indeed can ask and manifest whatever You feel like, but – always think about consequences. ¨Be carefull what You wish for¨ - this is THIS case.

I knew a lady who was desperate to meet a sporty,muscled guy with a big car. So she started to manifest her desire and indeed, some time later she met a sporty, muscled guy with a big car, who became her boyfriend. All his free time he was spending in the gym or taking care about his car. She got what she wanted. Was she happy with that? No.

Having a larger picture - ¨studying¨¨ all the apsects of the Universe and the way it ¨works¨ - will help You to avoid lots of deceptions. Such as ¨ i meditate and meditate and i still did not get that job/man/woman/house! That simply does not work!"

If its still "does not work",bthen there is a very big chance(a VERY big,i mean), that its not in Your life plan and its really better for You, that "it still does not work".

As pointed out above,there is a huge variety of aspects in our Life, in our Now and its important to have a deeper understanding, how it all Works together. And we have to be open "to study" if not it all, but then at least many facades of the Universe.

People with serious karmic debts, which can be presented in this life time as physical limitations or serious health issues, can spend an entire life "manifesting" health, but nothing will change, because the main Law of the Universe is the Law of Karma or the Law of Cause and Effect and there is no any meditation or manifestation, which can "free" You from Your debts. And if there are things to pay off, one will pay or balance them.

Thats why never be "upset" or sad or desperate, if manifestation "does not work". If something,no matter how hard we try,"does not work, there is a reason for that. And via this "does not work", Universe simply protects us from the consequences we are not aware about (there is always a larger vier from Above).

But if we really insist, according to the Law of Free Will, we might temporaly get,what we ask for. And likely if our wish comes from the ego, that will not make us happy and through the consequences, which will not be "nice", Universe will get us back on track.

The key-point of this chapter and of this book is to have an understanding, that Life/Universe is so much more, than our one-two favourite authors. That every authour is like a specialist in his/her own área. Like each doctor is a specialist in one área. And to get a larger picture and understanding, whats going on in our life and around us, how Universe ¨works¨, we should see ourselves as ¨therapists¨(using analogy with medics), who have general knowledges about human body (Life/Universe), but are not speacialising in anything particular. So when a therapist feels, that something ¨does not work¨, he knows the ¨problem area¨ and he sends a patient to the speacialist of that particular área.

The same is with Life. If manifestations for abundance dont work, then maybe its a past life/karmic debts issue and should be resolved in that área first.

So when ¨something does not work¨, dont rush with the conclusions, that ¨IT¨ does not work. Be grateful,that ¨it does not work¨, because via that way Life/Universe protects You from what is most likely is not ¨written¨ in Your life plan and therefore – is not for Your highest good.

When something, inspite of all the efforts, ¨does not work¨, ¨check¨ other áreas, why it might not be working. If, as mentioned above, You ¨work¨ on money issue and money still ¨dont come¨, then its likely karmic issue and one should check that área.

In this book i tryed to put together very different topics, as far as, in my point of view, exactly this variety helps to have a large picture and gives an understanding, why sometimes something ¨does not work¨, no matter how hard we try.

Because sometimes ¨only meditations¨, ¨only affirmations¨, ¨only past life regression¨ are not enough.

Sometimes - and most of the times - to change completely the direction of Your life, You have to make changes in many aspects of Your personal ¨matrix¨.

Meditations, the house and office free of clutter, the language You speak and the words You use, friends You have, self - discipline, understanding of the importance of moving forward... all this is important. EVERYTHING is important.

Having an understanding of these different aspects of Your personal ¨matrix¨ helps to have a larger picture, what and why is going on in Your life and around,where is the Key and how to ¨work¨ with that for the better changings.

Blessed be the Change.

Contents

CHAPTER 1

Nothing Is Permanent Or Static.

In this chapter i want to talk about our spiritual habits and rituals.

From the one hand if we have some rituals we like, it brings in our daily life discipline and the feeling of tranquility and safety,because day by day (or week by week;month by month,etc) we constantly repeat something and this "something" gives us an illusion,that everything is stable,everything is "as always".

But its really nothing more,than an illusion. I dont play with a negative context in here,which the word "illusion" can hold sometimes. I refer to the "illusion" as a substnace,that does not actually really exist.

Everything is energy and frequency that energy holds and therefore – nothing is ever static and permanent.

Life/Universe is constantly moving forward and expanding and each new second nothing is as it has been a second ago. And we are moving and expanding as well, even if we dont notice it.

Yes,we all have different speeds (according to our life plans and soul - ¨age¨),but we – as Life itself – are never static.

Keeping that in mind, i want to pay Your attention,that rituals and/or habbits, that were serving You a year (or more.or less) ago,probably dont serve You NOW anymore. And its for Your highest good to let them go and/or to update them and/or to change them for the new ones.

Discipline is good and necessary for growing and accomplishment thing(You can use word ¨success¨ here as well), but discipline is not a corset. Dont be afraid of letting something go only because You were doing it for quite a long time.

It was useful and served You according of that energy of Yours and according to the frequency of Life/Universe at that time,but it might be not serving You NOW.

Because You have changed. Even if You dont notice it, change and movement in You and therefore – in Life,happen ALL THE TIME.

Universe has expanded and everything vibrates on a different frequency now.

I want to share my own example.

During several months i was feeling a need to write every moring 10 things im blessed with.

I had this ritual while drinking my morning cup of tea and it felt so good and peaceful writing down and reading so many (most of the time i had much more than ten on my mind) things, i feel grateful for and im blessed with.

This morning ritual felt so right to start a day with! It

was a relatively (as far as i live in the southern city) cold period of the year and starting a day with a hot cup of tea counting my blessings was a wonderful moment for me. I simply loved it.

But few months later, when the weather started to get warmer,i began to realise,that instead of sitting at home this morning hour, i would rather spend time outside with my dog, enjoying the sun and the begining of the day. So i stopped to write down my blessings (but never stopped to count them and to be grateful) and started to enjoy my extra-time outside and I was feeling the same state of peace and tranquility which i had while i was practicing my "Morning Blessings Ritual".

I changed my morning ritual for another one,i moved forward with Life and i felt (and i feel) completely in the Flow.

Dont be attached to Your ritual-routine,even if that was making You feel good for years. Be open. Seek for the new things. Expand and Move with Life.

Nothing is ever static and permanent. Even if by the physical perception it seems so.

Keep in mind,that "the goal" is to evolve,to expand and to be happy; not to be stuck with "good old stuff".

Because there is always something better, what lays before us. Life/Universe loves us and wonderful surprises,gifts and opportunities are prepared for us already.

These gifts,surprises and opportunities are vibrating on a different frequency,higher than our current one (because nothing is static and everything moves,expands and evolves All The Time), so to get them,we have to change our energy/frequency,what can not be done if we are keep on doing the same things and if we are not moving forward.

Be open for all these new gifts and opportunities,that are ALREADY waiting for You.

Every day is a New day and new opportunity to grow and to expand.

There is nothing ¨bad¨ If You are getting benefits from ¨good old stuff¨, from ¨approved¨ things – from rituals/ spiritual routine You may be doing for years,but if You stick to the one particular practice and If You are not open for anything new,it means,that Your energy is in the stagnant state. Because,as discussed above, nothing is stagnant in Life/Universe and energy/frequency is constantly changing and if You are doing the same things year by year,it means,that You are not evolving, You are not moving forward with Life.

Its not about abandoning completely Your spiritual routine/things You love(even though sometimes its the case as well), its about updating them.

Its like with the romantic relationship. You can love and ¨enjoy¨ Your partner for years, but we know, that if we are not refreshing our relationship, it does not make us happy anymore till that degree, as it was in the beginning. So we try and we explore new things, new places, new destinations together(or separately) and that benefits relationship.

The same with rituals and our spiritual daily routine.

To be in the Flow with the rhytm of life, You need refreshments, You need updatings. And sometimes You need to make some cancellations. And to leave the past behind.

As with the relationships. Sometimes its useless (if not damaging and dangerous) to resurrect something, what is already dead and the only decisions one has to make – is to let it go with gratitude.

If You feel that some ritual/spiritual practice You used to have does not feel "right" anymore, then it means, its time to let it go. It served its purpose and was useful and beneficial for that particular period of time (time and space sequence) in the past. But the past is gone. Life moved forward and You moved with it. Your energy has changed and You just dont vibrate at the same frequency anymore and therefore – its time to learn and to apply new things.

As discussed above – it can be completely new "stuff" or it can be an "updated" routine/spiritual practice, but the Key thing here – is to move with the Flow of Life. And Life is never static.

How to understand that Your spiritual routine needs an update and how to do it?

The answer is as always simple – just tune into Yourself and listen to Your inner voice.

If You are starting to feel that You are doing Your rituals without the passion like it was in the beginning; if You are repeating it almost automatically and during the process Your thoughts wandering somewhere else ceaselessly (how to spend the weekend;what to wear,etc.),then its a clear indicator,that Your ritual is no longer serving You in the best way and needs – as mínimum – an update and a "cancellation" as máximum.

If You feel that some part of it is still useful,then think about the refreshment. Again- trust Your inner voice and ask for guidance.

Your heart and Your spiritual helpers already have suggestions for You,so just ask and listen. No need to explain them Your issue extensively – they already "know" the situation.

Ask simple questions. For example - " What should I do to make this ritual/practice work better for me?"" or " Shall i let it go?", " What are the new things i shall try?". Just ask and be open and receptive for the answers and guidance.

If You are on a high frequency state and Your energy is as pure as it can be according to the circumstances (the physical body is not abused with meat, alcohol, toxic substances), trust the first thought, that came to Your mind.

If You feel that the answer is there,but somehow You still cant figure it clearly out, ask Your heart/Your helpers to be more precise.

If You feel, that the answer is just to take a break from all Your rituals, then follow this advice.

Spiritual people (myself included) have a tendency to be "too spiritual" sometimes. And in some periods of life the best option is to enjoy some down to earth pleasures.

After a break You will feel refreshed and will "come back" to Your spiritual life with new energy and excitement.

Having a break is also moving forward, because thats what Your essence needs in this particular "now" and

if You follow Your needs, You follow The Flow Of Life.
Because YOU are Life.

So…

Listen to Your heart and keep on moving .

CHAPTER 2

Karma

We all know (or have heard) this word ¨karma¨. And many of us have at least an idea of karma.

But…

what is actually ¨karma¨?

Most of us, including myself, were raised with a very vague idea of karma. In my case it also always had a negative context.

For many years i saw karma as something ¨bad¨, whats lying over people´s shoulders with enormously heavy weight. But this image doesn´t reflect the truth.

Let me give You an example, which helped me to understand, what really karma is.

So imagine Yourself on the road and with a backpack. This backpack is Your ¨karma¨. While walking Your life path/¨road¨ we constantly pick up and put in our backpack different stuff. We also constantly take out different, ¨worked out¨ stuff. ¨Karma-stuff¨. But WHAT we pick up and what put in our backpack – that depends totally and ONLY on us. Its OUR way,its OUR backpack and no one has right or even a possibility to touch our backpack and/or to put something in it.

We are the Owners. No one else. So we have an absolutely free choice, what we fill our bag with. We can fill it with stones and dirt – things, which will be difficult to carry on and which will ¨bother¨ other ¨travellers¨ next to us. Or we can pick up and fill our backpack with beautiful flowers and precious gifts and wonderful surprises, which Universe always has for us. And in this case Your backpack, being so easy and nice to carry on, will be a pleasure not only for You, but also for everyone around.

The choice is always Yours.

The key thing here, that karma doesn't necessary has to be ¨a bad¨ thing. Karma – is EVERYTHING. For example, that i live in the nice district in front of the sea – its also my karma. All the good things in Your life – its Your karma.

Some people work in noisy crowded offices, the others - doing the same(or almost the same) things in the sunny terraces or at the beach (in our internet-epoque these options are possible).... So WHY its like that?

Answers could be different – sometimes it has nothing to do with karma, but with self-discipline and determination in study, but sometimes – yes,its karma. ¨Good¨ karma from the previous life-times.

I want to pay Your attention to the important point - DONT confuse karma with laziness.

If You were born in financially poor family and from

the very early days You were struggling for money, then yes - the beginning of Your life - journey is karma, also based on Your life lesson.

BUT.

If You see this initially given circumstances as an excuse for Your stagnation, spending days on the sofa, watching TV and complaining about Your karma, then... it has NOTHING to do with karma. Its laziness in all its glory.

Karma is not something that You cant see or feel. In my point of view, karma is tangible. One can feel the lightness or heaviness of life circumstances and/or situations, one can feel people around her or him, therefore - one can ¨feel¨ karma.

Keep in mind, that all what You have in Your life - like,for example, a nice appartment in the nice district or a good, reliable partner - its also Your karma. You ¨earned¨ it in Your previous life times.

And if You, having what You have, feel, that life is unfair to so many people around You, who dont have what You have, dont rush for the pity and the most important - dont rush to give everything away in order ¨to share¨ and ¨ to be nice¨. You deserve to have and to enjoy what You have absolutely to the same degree, that other people ¨deserve¨ what they dont have.

Here is an important moment - dont take it to the extreme degree, when one passes by people, who really need help and whom You CAN help (and who will be grateful for that. not everyone needs and wants Your help, remember that. Some chose to suffer and to complain).

For instance, in India, where the concept of karma

is widely known, people sometimes can literally pass by people on the streets, who need help (in case of accidents, for example) with ¨well,its their karma¨ - explanation. Nothing to do with that. And its more likely that in the next life someone will also pass them by - we receive,what we give.

We are here to share and to help each other. And if You see, that someone needs help and You can help, go for it. Especially in the cases of accidents, for example, when ambulance is still not there and You CAN help(simple starring in the crowd around - this is NOT help). Dont pass by by comforting Yourself with ¨its her/his karma¨. This postion becomes YOUR karma as well.

BUT.

If, for example, You are dealing with friends and/or relatives, who constantly ask You for help with the same things and situations and You just starting to feel tired of that never ending help.... Even if money/time dont cost You a lot, but what if You just dont feel good about it anymore...?

Everything has its limit.

This includes ¨help¨. Help has its limit. And If You feel this limit, its time to stop this help NOW. The feeling of this limit is an indicator, that with Your help You started to interfer peoples karma and life lessons, they have to learn and pass by THEMSELVES. By doing everything or most of THEIR work, You actually take their karma and their life lessons in Your ¨backpack¨. Dont You have enough of Your stuff?

There is more here. If You constantly do something what other person has to do by her/himself, in this case

You dont let this person to fulfill her/his life plan and to "work out" her/his karma and there is a good chance, that she or he will have to incarnate next time with the very same life lessons. How does that sound? Will You both feel super happy there, "upstairs", when You will be analising Your former life and chosing the next one?

Another very important aspect of any kind of help - YOU CANT GIVE WHAT YOU DONT HAVE. Or You can give only what You have. As You prefer.

It means, that Your help will be REAL help ONLY if Your own life and comfort will not be "damaged" and Your help will be on the frequency of the pure joy to serve. NOT on the frequency of pity and/or duty. This very important to realise and to APPLY. Because in the eyes of the Universe its INTENTION what is really matters and counts.

There are many rich (and not that rich) people who participate in charity, but it doesn't look like that this brings them inner peace and happiness. Why is that so? The INTENTION is the key. If one helps, because one "has to do it", because "everyone does it", because " people will see how good and generous i am"etc., this help comes from the ego, which orients on the fear of what people say/think and what comes from the ego dont makes us happy.

Sooner or later You will start to feel tired and drained, You will start to feel that You give "too much" or that You give, what's actually "Yours". This kind of "help" holds low energy and there will come the moment, when You will feel overhelmed with Your "rescue mission". If this rings a bell, the best option is to stop any "help" immediately. No matter what and how much You have, if You give it with the ¨closed¨ heart... - You DONT help. You actually make it worse. And for Yourself and for the others (taking in Your ¨backpack¨ whats not Yours¨).

BUT.

Even if You have little and You are full of joy by sharing this ¨little¨ - then Your help is REAL.

Always keep in mind - we all deserve what we have . It is ¨earned¨ by You in Your previous lives and its the consequence of Your decisions and choices in the current one and You have all the rights to fully enjoy what You have. Our original nature is to share and to help, but if You dont feel good by doing that, then its a sign that You do it with the wrong situation and with the wrong person.

If You give the last what You have and the quality of Your life ¨suffers¨ by giving and sharing, then You give ¨what You dont have¨. Like in the airplane - first put Your mask on YOURSELF, then put it on Your child. Here is the same. Only when You have enough for Yourself, You cant start to help others.

What does it mean - ¨to have enough for Yourself¨? Whats the definition of that ¨enough¨?

You have enough, when You sleep enough, when You eat enough, when You relax enough and when You have enough of money to make You feel GOOD. Your help is real help, when You have enough of all of these aspects.

For instance, if You live in the small appartment in the touristically attractive city/place and have enough space just for Yourself and Your family members/ relatives/friends constantly ¨pass by¨ for a week(s) during their vacation, playing with that You live in that nice location and ¨ we are family¨ and ¨we are friends¨ etc....

and You keep on saying ¨yes¨ in order to be ¨nice¨instead of being honest and say ¨NO¨? ¨No¨ - because having guests You just dont feel comfortable at Your own home and You need space for Yourself. If this sounds familiar to You, then its time to stop being ¨nice¨ and to start to be honest. You have all the rights to enjoy YOUR place (no matter how big it is) and not to share it with anyone else(yes, even if its a friend or a family member). Everything You have, You have for a reason. And what they dont have - they dont have it for a reason as well. Constant help to the same people with the same issues prevent them from growth, fulfilling their life plans and working out their karma.

So how to understand if You REALLY need to help in some particular situation or its better to bless it and to walk away? The answer is ALWAYS short and simple - Your inner voice.

Ask Yourself HONESTLY - Do You really want to help? Does it feel RIGHT? Or You feel like more an obligation and/or pity is on the stage? If Your inner voice tells You NOT to do it, then DONT. No matter what Your mind tell You.... just dont do it. Your inner voice always knows the truth, the truth of following Your own life plan and letting the others to follow their. And when we act not according our life plan, that never makes us happy and that never goes to the right direction. Dont let Yourself be trapped by ¨to help - is a good thing to do¨. NOTHING is never good for You if YOU dont feel good about it.

And no matter, what other people say. Whay they think or say about You - its not Your business(James Van

Praagh). "Your business" is to live YOUR life and to work on YOUR life lessons.

You are responsible for Your own karma, not for anyone's else. And You deserve what You have. Like anyone else.

CHAPTER 3

The Importance Of Your Clean Space

Everything is energy.

Look around.

What kind of energy surrounds You? How Your place looks like? What Your home tells about You?

No matter how many spiritual/self-help books You have read and how many life-changing seminars/ workshops/retreats You have attended,but if Your place looks neglected and untidy,thats an indicator,that You dont actually apply what You are reading about.

To read is not enough. ¨ To know¨ means ¨to apply¨. If one does not apply what ones reads about,it means that one just likes to read. There is difference between ¨spiritual¨ people and people who read spiritual books.

Your home, Your place tells right away if You just read a book or if You apply what You read about.

The essence of spirituality is authenticity and pure

energy. Till what degree Your place is authentically YOU? What it consists of?

If Your home is a mix of any sort of energies, ALL that energy influences Your energy field," distracts" Your own energy and its very difficult for You to feel where is "You" and where is "not You".

Many of us have many objects at home,that dont represent us,that dont reflect "what" we are, but we still keep them in order to please those,who gave them to us or just because "i bought it 20 years ago in that trip!". If our homes are full of objects and things,that have nothing to do with the current versión of us now, that does not allow us to grow, to expand and to move forward with the speed we could easily move if all these things were not in our lives anymore.

Meditation and/or affirmation work, which is made in the littered room DOES NOT have the same effect if it takes place in the tidy space. Everthing is energy and energy of the objects around You affects Your energy work. Yes,everything is inside You. And... everything is connected.

"Inside" is connected with the ""outside".

So again. Take a look around. Look carefully and think/feel,what object/thing in the room does not reflect Your essence anymore? If it belongs to the past,take it out of Your life. It occupies the space of the thing/object (person/situation/opportunity) from Your future. And as we know,nothing new can come into our lives,while the place for that new is still busy with the old stuff. Thats the one side of the coin.

The other side is, that,while Your place is not "clean"

enough, spiritual helpers who's vibration is much higher,than the human ones and who already ¨make an effort¨ to low their energy to communicate with us,they simply are not able to get through the clutter You have around You. The dimensión we currently live here on Earth (3d dimensión) is already dense enough for those who are willing to help,to support us from the higher realms and clutter around us does not help them in that.

Respect not only Yourself, but also those,whom You are communicating with. Be it another human being or a spiritual helper. When You invite friends at Your place, most likely You clean Your appartment,before they come.

If You want to be constantly ¨online¨ with Your spiritual helpers, be ready to provide the appropriate environment for Your ¨guests¨. Asking for guidance and help sitting in the room full of clutter will not lead to the great results.

Clean house is not only a very simple gesture to show that You respect Yourself. Its also Your respect to Universe and all those who are willing to help You.

We spend at home mínimum 8 hours. Even those of us who are very busy,they are at home at least for sleeping. In what energy do You sleep? You can spend the whole day at the spiritual workshop surrounded by high energy,but still You come back home in the evening. You come back to Your ¨normal¨ energy. And its not that meditation once a day that ¨counts¨. EVERYTHING counts. Because everything – is energy. And Your energy field (and therefore – YOU) consists of every kind of energy You are surrounded during the day,day by day. And night by night.

The same with the people You invite to Your place. Keep in mind – every person is a mix of energy and information. What energy and information Your guests add to the energy of Your place and therefore – to YOU? If there is some ¨weird¨ feeling about some friend or relative, You have all the rights not to let that person to cross Your doormat. Your place is YOUR space. And You have all the rights to be at home in YOUR energy. And this is vitally important. If You are never in Your energy, You are a very easy target for influence,because Your energy field is not strong enough due to many energies around.

Ideally Your place should be a ¨recharge¨- space for Your energy field. And this means,thats people, things and objects You have around You at home should be at the same frequency, that You are.

There is another extreme when people cant stop cleaning the space around them,but that already a psychological issue. Extremes are never good and no need to live in the appartments,that resemble zen monasteries.

The same goes about the office space or any other space where You spend Your working hours. Your energy field absorbes the energy of Your working desk. So how does that desk (or any other space You work in) looks like? Is it full of clutter or neat and tidy?

Of course, You are not responsable for the entire office building and/or for the entire company,but you do responsable for Your own table. Make it nice and clean and does not matter how the tables of the others look like. Think about Yourself and YOUR life. Because - remember - YOU is EVERYTHING (Your working space as well) and everything counts.

Olga Kharitonova

There are many useful books about organising private and working space(and not all of them are ¨spiritual¨). My favourite ones are from Denise Linn. But books are not necessary. The most important that You feel GOOD, that You feel ¨fresh¨ at home.

That You have free space for the enter of the new and better things,which are already on the way to Your life :).

CHAPTER 4

Friends

According to Anais Nin ¨each friend represents a world in us, a world possibly not born until a friend arrives. And its only by this meeting that a new world is born¨.

Lets take a look at this beautiful adage through spiritual perspective and say,that by meeting a new friend, a new world is not born, but new world awakens,as far as everything is already within. And no one can ¨open¨ anything inside us if we already dont have it.

So what kind of worlds our friends can awake in us and what is actually ¨a friend¨?

We consider a friend as someone who is ¨always there¨ and wishes only the best for us. And indeed, ideally it should be really like that. But we live in a wonderful and beautiful world. Not in an ideal one And guess what? Better for us. Otherwise,how could we progress and master our life lessons if everything is just so damn perfect around?

Friends,as any other persons in our lives,have ¨a

purpuse¨. They are here to have fun with us,to support us in life challenges and new beginnings,to cheer us up and so on. Thats true, indeed. But its also just a part of the story.

If we are talking about healthy friendship,it is really so. And its a real blessing and a great feeling to enjoy a friendship like that – when people have fun,support and encourage each other. But lets face the truth – not every friendship is like that.

There are friendships,which are based not on the mutual support,encouragement and desire to grow and to move forward together,but on permanent complains about life and the others.

And this kind of friendship teaches us an ultimatelly important life lesson – a lesson to say NO.

If You are a person,who is interested in moving forward with The Flow Of Life,but some people around You,whom You used to call ¨friends¨ are just keep on talking and expierencing the same stuff all the time,these friendships are pulling You back. Some people are not interested in growing. And more than that – they are not interested that the others grow either. They are NOT interested tha YOU grow.

If You think/feel that this is the case – its time to think GOOD,if these friends belong to Your future.

There is another aspect in here,too. Its also posible,that according to Your pre-birth life plan,some souls have chosen to be Your ¨friends¨ to teach You the lesson of saying NO and to let people/past go.

As we know,the most important of our life lessons we learn ¨through¨ our loved ones. And the lesson to care about Yourself, Your own growth and therefore - a lesson to say NO to everything (and everybody),what does not serve this purpose – is a lesson that is hardly ever learned in an easy way.

Its easy (not to everybody though) to say NO to a stranger on the street,but saying NO to someone,who we consider as our friend,seems sometimes as a difficult ¨task¨. And exactly this task is needed to be done.

In the eyes of the Universe a stranger on the street is the same ¨teacher¨ to You as Your friend. And if You are able to stand up for Yourself and Your time and Your money (in case if some beggers are constantly asking You for money and You give it out of the feeling of the obligation and/or guilt) with the starnger on the street(or an annoying neighbour,who,for example, always complains about the life),so the same You have to be able to do with a person,whom You call a friend.

In fact, ¨no one is Your enemy and no one is Your friend. But everyone is Your teacher¨(indian proverb).

Being in friendship,which doesn´t meet Your needs and pulls You back from Your Path is failing Your life lesson to say NO to everything and to everybody,what doesn´t serve Your highest good.

You will always feel that Your friendship is ¨expired¨ and its time to walk separate ways,but being raised in the society,where its appreciated and honored to be ¨friends¨ with complete ¨strangers¨ just because You went together to the kindergarden,school,University,dance class etc. And trying to be (or being) a ¨nice¨ person, You will be probably feeling ¨bad¨ to leave this past behind.

If this rings a bell, then consider the following :

NOW You are NOT the same person You were in the kindergarden (well,lets hope You are not:))). You have changed and You have changed a lot. You have different goals now, different interests,different priorities... YOU are different. The same as Your best kindergarden/school friend. Now its another person(likely). And there is a chance that both of You are pretending to be the same,when You have met,because thats the only one way to maintain ¨the friendship¨ - to ¨be¨ the past. And to talk about the past (happens a lot with school/university friends,who are not that close anymore).

And it takes an effort to be brave enough and to face the truth – its not the same friendship anymore. And maybe its not a friendship at all. And what it looks like now – is a waisting Your precios time and energy on something,what is not ¨You¨anymore. Just because You were playing together,when You were 4(14,24) doesn´t mean,that You are close people NOW.

Dont get me wrong – im not talking,that any friendship,which lasts many years,doesn´t serve You. Thats not the case. If You have friends You know for decades and You feel real intimacy with them, You support and encourage each other... THIS friendship nourishes YOU and thats great. Thats really great to share wonderful memories together,to know that THATS the person You can trust,because her/his support and presence in Your life is proven by years. This kind of friendship is pure blessing and gift.

But we are talking about cases,when some ¨friends¨ are present in our lives ONLY because they were present there during some time (school,university,etc.) 10, 20 or more years ago. If You still enjoy Your company together, You can easily skip,whats written below. If not, lets talk.

To grow and to move forward we need new situations,new circumstances and new people in our lives. We can't learn anything new if we read the same book all the time. Yes,we have our favourite books we enjoy reading and rereading ("old friends"). But we have also have spent time with the books,which were in our hands only because,for example,we had a vacation and could not get anything else, than this book or someone else gave it to us as a present and maybe it was not such a bad reading indeed,but You have read it and You know,that You will never open it again ("friends" from the past). Do You regret,that the book served its purpose and its time to let it go? Of course,not.

The same is with the people.

Dont be afraid to admit to Yourself, that some people dont belong nor to Your presence nor to Your future anymore. They belong to Your PAST. And even though You have shared great moments together,if NOW You have nothing else to do,except,than talking about these very same moments all the time,then its time to let it go. And to free the space for new people to come. For the people,who will enrich Your life in a new way and who will add new, fresh energy into Your energy field.

Listen – always – to Your inner voice. If this voice is telling You,that this friendship is already "expired",then dont feel sad or "bad" to let it go. I did it several times in my life and now i feel nothing, except gratitude for the fact and for those people,who were in my life and with whom we had wonderful time together, with whom we learned new things and that now past is not holding us back.

If You feel that when You are together with Your friend and there is nothing else to talk about,then to discuss the past ("...and do You remember?"), then be honest with Yourself and ask Yourself a simple question: Would You rather be in some other place and/or with some other people (or alone),than here,with THIS person,talking about things You are not interested in and pretending to be a person You are not (a person,You were 10,20,30 etc. years ago)?

If the answer is YES, then dont be in a rush to give a positive respond,when You will be invited by this person next time. Value Your time. You dont owe anything to anybody and You have all the rights to say NO, when You really feel like to do it.

Value Your past, honour it, be thankful, but dont "feed" it with Your energy again and again.

Your Present and Future need it.

Chapter 5

Meditation & Past Life Regressions

In our western world we have a misconseption of meditation.

Many people hearing word ¨meditation¨ immediately have an image of a monk in the orange robe sitting in the Lotus-position somewhere on the top of the hill. Yes, indeed, one can wear an orange robe, sit in the Lotus-position and ¨meditate¨ on the top of the hill.

But what is actually ¨meditation¨ and if Lotus-position (and the orange robe. And the hill) is really necessarily required?

Meditation is coming back home. To home which is inside us. To come back to this home You dont need any special robe, You dont need any special place and in most of the cases You dont need any special position.

Meditation is Your own space of YOUR truth and YOUR authenticity, which is available to You anywhere and at any time.

We all have busy lives and most of us share their home living with someone. In this case its not easy sometimes ¨to find a tranquil place where You will be undisturbed¨ as many meditations books and CD´ advise. Its not easy to find ¨a tranquil place¨ when You are a mother of a newborn, for example or You live in a numerous family and square meters are in a nigh demand. Not always You can just close the door and say ¨dont disturb¨. But always You CAN find 2 minutes just to close Your eyes, make a deep breath and say/think/feel whatever makes You feel comfortable and safe. My favourite one is ¨Home is inside me¨. But it can be absolutely anything what makes YOU feel comfortable.

> Love is inside me
> Safety is inside me
> Tranquility is inside me
> Strength is inside me
> Determination is inside me

Just to name a few and to give an example. This could also be :

> Im safe
> Im lovable
> Im strong

Whatever makes a click for YOU, will work for YOU. And yes, these 2 minutes, when You close Your eyes (or maybe not), when You turn to Yourself and when You speak to Yourself and when You HEAR Yourself – THIS is meditation. Yes,simple as that.

Of course,its only ONE type of meditation as far as there are many, but yes -its meditation as well. Coming back "home" - to YOURSELF, to the true, authentic YOU – this IS meditation.

Yes,for some of us room with a closed door and time just for ourselves sounds like a luxury, but lets be honest - each and everyone of us can find these 2 minutes. It can be even in the rest room. Obviously, WC doesnt have such a nice view as the monastery on the hill top, but thats not about the view. Its about YOU. About Your time to come back to YOUR home, which is always with You. Inside YOU. Meditation is nothing else, than turning back to Your inner voice, which used to be in the flight-mode in our busy days and daily routine.

Everything is very individual and its not proper to affirm, that there is one-size-fits-all meditation and one-size-fits-all meditation timing and time.

Thousand years ago monks used to meditate for hours early in the morning on the tops of the hills. We are not monks who live thousand years ago. Universe/ Life/Everything constantly expands, evolves and moves forward. Current reality consists of constantly updating "Here" and "Now". And everyone of us has her/his unique " Here" and "Now". Thats why, what was right for some monk a thousand years ago, probably is not right for YOU now.

As far as You are reading these pages, its likely that Your days are not organised that way, that each and every single day You have the very same things to do. Especially if You live a family life, which implies different activities with children and other family members. And that means that not every day You have time for even a half an hour meditation. And there is nothing wrong with that. Again – meditation is coming back to Yourself, to Your inner home and space. And there are days when You feel like to be ¨home¨ more and there are days when You feel like to be ¨at home¨ less.

But for our well being its beneficial to be at least some time ¨at home¨. And if not daily, then at least once in a while.

There are different types of meditations and if You never meditated before, then a guided meditation is probably the best option for You. Without practice of calming Your mind, its very easy to be distracted by different kind of thoughts in the beginning. Guided meditation will help You to stay on track.

There is a huge ammount of guided meditations, so its normal if You will feel sort of lost in doing the first steps. There is only one advice, which is suitable for every situation including this one - listen to Your inner voice. If You feel drawn to some particular meditation, pick up that one. Even if Your mind is trying to tell You, that You have nothing to do with that ¨issue¨.

For example.

Feeling drawn to the mediation which ¨works¨ on the inner confidence topic, You mind could try to tell You,that You are confident person and why should You work on that? But if You FEEL,that its the Right meditation,pick that one up. It means that exactly in this particular Now (time and space sequence), You need exactly this work.

Think about this. Your energy field from time to time - according to what is going on in Your life and

Your circumstances - has "weak" points. These points need some special "medicines", which are designed exactly for this particular points. And Your inner voice (Your heart / Your Higher Self) always knows, which points need "medicines".

Just like with the physical body. If there is a pain/ uncomfortable feeling in some part of the body, one works exactly with that particular part and one - if needed - uses a medicine for that part.

The same is with the meditations. If You pick up one without thinking too much, just because it feels right, then its THIS mediation, that You need Now. You will never make a mistake following Your inner guidance. Even if You dont quite understand,why its This one, trust - that exactly the one You need Now.

Its not necessary to meditate in "official" meditation Lotus-position. Meditation – is work with Your Higher Self and Higher Self doesn't have physical body. The most important here is to find this tranquil time for Yourself and not to spend this time struggling keeping Your back straight. Relaxing meditations (probably thats the best option to start with) does not even require Your fully conscience presence. It means its OK if You fall asleep. Dont blame Yourself – Your Higher Self will do the "work" anyway.

Thats not the case of manifestation meditations,though. If You want to manifest something, its better to be in the conscious state so You can directly send You energy to the desired outcome. In this case yes, its better, if You sit up straight – this will prevent You from falling asleep(likely).

But when it goes about relax or healing mediation

"strict" positions are not necessary. Its not possible fully relax, if one is constantly trying to keep in mind to sit in the "right" position.:)

So - again - chose whats better for YOU. And keep in mind – meditation is work with Your Higher Self (or "sub/unconscious mind" how we used to call it in the western world), not with Your back muscles. Higher Self does not have physical body, so it doesnt matter which position You take in most of the cases. The most important, that You do find time to meditate. Always listen to Yourself and dont meditate out of "obligation".

If You meditation practice takes some part in Your daily routine, but in some days You dont feel to do it, then dont. Then it must be reasons why should not meditate in that particular day. Important point – here i talk not about short " home comeback", which i mentioned earlier. This kind of meditations are meant to reassure and comfort You and to make You "remember", that everything You need is already within, that there is no place for fear. But here i talk about deep inner work meditations, which sometimes need their special "moment" and if You dont feel that moment, but want to meditate only because "i didnt meditate today yet,i have to!", then its not the right thing to do. Always listen whats Your inner voice tells You.

Some meditations (energy work) need time to be "absorbed" and to "adjust" Your energy field according to the new frequencies and in this case You may need several days of no meditations at all. Because if You put on "layers" of deep inner work/transformation one on another, Your energy field will "flip" by this new energy/information, which were "imprinted" in Your energy "matrix". Its like to eat several delicious meals at the very same time - You will not be fully enjoy the taste and more likely You will not enjoy Your meal.

Here is the same.

If, lets say, every day You do deep inner work, but on the different aspects of You, then Your energy field does not have time to fully integrate these new aspects You are working on. And the "system failure"" can happen. In this case, a part of that Your inner work would be sort of "collapsed" under the big ammount of the new information, physically You can feel tired, weak or maybe even lightly sick.

Another moment is, that if You do meditate regularly, its important that the space where You meditate (if You have a special one) is free of different clutter. Everything is energy. Whats energy around You when You do Your healing inner work,for example? Does it contribute to the healing work or does it "disturb" Your energy field? Remove things/images You dont feel good about (its good to do it not only from the room,but from Your life as well),let the meditation space be free of anything what does not give You positive or neutral vibes. It should be a place where You feel good even without any meditation.

Remember, that nothing new can come in our lives, if we dont free the space for it first. If You are surrounded by old "stuff" while trying to change Your consciousness, You will not get desirable results quickly.

Free the space for new consciousness first.

Dont overhelm Yourself with different kind of meditations. Dont meditate only because You "have to". But always find 2 mins for Your "coming back home".

PAST LIFE REGRESSION.

There are many exellent books about past life issues and past life regressions (Michael Newton, Brian Weiss, Trutz Hardo just to name a few autors), so there is no need to repeat and its not a past life issue book either.

But its important to know, that one should not have a fear of doing a regression if there is an interest in that. Universe and all spiritual helpers and Teachers LOVE You and You would never be shown something You are not ready to see and to perceive. If the fear of seeing ¨something bad¨ is too big, You simply would not be shown anything at all.

But… dont be afraid..:) Dont be afraid to know YOUR own story, YOUR own track… You are here. You are alive. Its all PAST.

Have a good journey :)

CHAPTER 6

Stagnation Vs Patience

From the early childhood many of us have been told ¨to be patient¨. ¨To be patient¨ with our family members and friends, ¨to be patient¨ with our partners, ¨to be patient¨ with our children and so forth.

And in many cases this so called ¨patience¨ leaded to unhappy and dull lives. As mínimum. And as máximum this ¨patience¨ could lead to the death(¨patience¨ with a violent partner,for example). Extreme patience is dangerous.

If You are constantly patient in abusive and toxic relationships, then day by day You are denying, who You truly are. You are denying Your own unique essence and this denial always has consequences as physical and mental issues.

Constant patience in the relationships where You are not valued, Your needs are not met and You are not heard, this kind of ¨patience¨(not to call ¨masochism¨)

leads to chronic fatigue, stress and discomfort,which can transform into severe depression.

This ¨patience¨ is not patience at all. Its self-denial and self-sacrifice. And its a vaste of Your precious life and time.

Its a stagnation. Stagnation,where no one and nothing moves. And as we know, Life never stops and always move forward.

For all of us, who are naturally ¨givers¨ and caretakers is ultimately important not to miss that line, when patience transforms into stagnation. Because this line devides Your life in two completely different lives.

Patience is a life lesson,which HAS future. Stagnation is always a vaste of time and more important – stagnation is always lost opportunities. Because while You are in Your stagnant state (while You are ¨patient¨), You are not moving with The Flow Of Life and opportunities exist ONLY in the Flow. Opportunities are not stagnant, opportunities are not extremely ¨patient¨. They exist in one particular and perfcet time and space sequence.

Life/Universe is not stagnant and ¨patient¨, it constantly moves and evolves.

As the opportunities and gifts which are prepared for You, they are not going to be there forever. Everything has its limit. And if You dont take the opportunities which are in front of You here and now,there is a big chance that You will never have them again. The time is always NOW.

When You are stagnant – too patient – You miss this Magic Flying Now, which is Life itself.

It easily can be seen in the example of romantic relationships.

Yes, its absolutely right to be patient with our partners and successful relationships are almost always have their turmoil times. The thing is, that these turmoil times pass by and You finally start to enjoy real fulfilled relationships or You constantly live in the turmoil mode, but trying "to be patient" as "good" and "nice" people have to be.

In this case its a way to nowhere. Because staying in the relationship, where You constantly have "to be patient" instead of being happy, You are preventing from happiness not only Yourself, but also Your partner. Because in this very moment, when one or both of you are struggling "to be patient", there is a man or woman "waiting" for You and/or for Your partner. That man or woman, who suits You perfect without any struggle in this particular time and space sequence. But being stagnant in Your struggle "to be patient", You just don't have any chance to let that person to come in into Your life. Nothing and nobody new can come into our lives, while the space is still busy with the old "stuff". Your "patience", transformed into stagnation, doesn't let You to take an opportunity to be happy. And does not give this opportunity to Your partner.

The line between patience and stagnation is NOT fine. When You are not happy, You dont feel The Flow Of Life and You are "out" of this Flow. Nothing new happens with You and to You. New doors are not opening, new opportunities are not appearing. You are "too patient" with Universe and Universe is "too patient" with You.

We receive, what we give. And if we "give" patience (which Universe already sees as a stagnation), then we will receive only ""patience" (stagnation in our lives).

It means while You are too patient to live Your fulfilled

life, Universe is too patient to give You the opportunities to do so. Because for Universe its just a waste of energy to give something to somebody, who is constantly ¨patient¨ instead of do some movements. And Universe gives opportunities and giftes to those ones, who are not ¨to patient¨, because in this case energy is not ¨wasted¨, its not in a stagnant/patient state, but moves and evolves. And thats what All this about.

People often wonder, why when they are so ¨nice¨ and ¨patient¨ with their friends, partners,family members and collegues, this ¨patience¨seems only makes the situation worse. Because there is a big confusión between patience and stagnation. People miss the line, where patience transforms into stagnation and where the life lesson of patience transforms into the life lesson of saying NO. Saying NO to the stagnation and saying YES to moving forward and embracing new life opportunities and life gifts.

Stagnation not only stops YOU from being creator of Your own life.

As far as we are all connected, it also influence and stops people around You. The best way to make Your life and therefore – a world a better place, is to walk Your talk and not by ¨bla-bla- teaching¨, but by being a living example of Your words.

If You are reading this book, its more likely that You live a mindful life and the conversations You have with Your Friends and/or family members are not shallow ones. You probably talk about the importance of knowing and exploring Yourself and life; that we are here to grow and to learn.

But we cant grow and learn, if we are surrounded by people with whom we should be always "nice" and "patient". Extreme patiece is a stagnation for the both sides of the relationships. It blocks Your energy and it blocks new situations and life expierences, which are passing by - because Universe/Life is not stagnant – and which could be a part of YOUR moving and expansión.

And if with Your Friends and/or family members You talk about the importance of inner work and moving forward, but at the same time, You and Your way of living dont reflect Your words, then no one is moving here. These conversations is a waste of energy and it goes to nowhere.

To know – means to APPLY.

And if You talk about things, but dont "live" them… then You just talk. Its a waste of time. And – again – its a waste of energy.

There is another trick in here.

If You really walk Your talk, if You are a living example and proof of moving forward, but the people around You just eagerly nod on Your words… dont be patience with them too long.

Yes, every change requires time. Including time for You to explain, what do You want and/or need and which direction You are thinking to take.

And time for the other person to absorb this information and to decide, if he/she/they are ready to move with You and/or to support You. Its a big or even radical change and a person definitely needs more time (cases of having or not having children; moving to other places etc.), even though deep inside she/he feels the answer almost immediately. But of course, You cant demand life-changing decisions right away and in this case time to reflect should be taken.

But the question is - how much time?

If You are clear about, what You want and the other person is just procrastinating his/her decisión, then there is no need and no sense to be patient anymore. Because the chance that You are already in the stagnant state and losing Your new opportunities is high.

Stop and dont be patient with the people, who dont have and will never have the same speed that You have. Dont let Your patience and ¨being nice¨ transform into stagnation and stop You from the life You want and deserve to have.

Know, remember and FEEL the difference.

Patience is a life lesson/state, which HAS future.

Stagnation is always a waste of time and lost opportunities.

CHAPTER 7

Talents And Creativity

We are all gifted.

No exeptions.

Each and every one of us has talents and gifts he/she came here on Earth to share. And these gifts and talents are not really ¨ours¨. They come and express ¨through¨ us as a part of the Divine and they are ¨given¨ to us not to be hidden or shared with a few loved ones. They are given to bring the Light and the Divine sparkle in the hearts of many people.

But what happens, when we are too shy or too modest (or too lazy) to express the talents and gifts we were meant to express and to share with the others? We start to feel incomplete and unfulfilled. Its this creative energy, which is within, that does not find a way out, starts ¨to bother¨ us inside out, so we finally start to move.

If You are talented and/or have special skills, but You

dont express Yourself and You dont share them with the world, You... You steal from the other people .

Let me repeat this important moment – If You dont express Yourself and dont share Your gifts and talents, which were given to You to be expressed through YOU – You steal from the people around You.

We all deserve what we have. Our gifts and talents included. Its our legacy from the past lives, which multilplies, transforms and grows with each life time. And the creative energy we have is also ¨earned¨ and given to make life here, on Earth, more bright and colourful.

Think about this. Im sure there are moments in Your life, probably at the end of the busy day, when You feel tired, grumpy, irritated.... and suddenly You open Your Facebook/Instagram page and You see some funny post or photo and that makes You smile and You already feel better. Happens to You, right?

And now imagine,that at the end of that very same day You come back home, You open Your Facebook/Instagram page and .... nothing. Nothing. All what You see is boring ¨normal¨ pics and oficial news. No one made an effort to express her/his creativity; no one posted something funny and/or creative; nothing inspiring and uplifting either. Everyone was too shy or too modest or too lazy.

And here is the result – dull and boring world.

Dont be too shy or too modest (and obviously,not too lazy) to open Your talents and to make the world brighter and better place. If You are given something, You are given that for a reason (everything happens for a reason). And this reason is pretty simple – You are given that to SHARE.

Dont let modesty or shyness to steal/to take not only from Yourself,but also from all those, who are around You.

Many of us (myself included) from our early days were taught "to be modest", not to "show off", "to be humble" and so on. In other words, we were taught to be small.

Now its the time to FORGET it all. Because being talented and gifted has nothing to do with being "small".

Modesty is a good thing,when You have nothing to say or nothing to show. But when You are gifted and talented, modesty is not the right partner to rely on. Modesty and shyness can fetter Your talent and bury it so deep, that it would never see a day light and would never have a chance to open up and to shine for those, who need it. Who need exactly that form of creativity, which was given exactly through YOU.

We all chose our life script before coming back here on Earth. And we carefully chose not only the life path we are going to go through in order to master our lessons, but we also carefully chose "things" we "take" into our new incarnation. And these "things" are also our virtues, gifts and talents. And we embody these "things" not to shine only for ourselves and not to constantly remind the others around, how smart,beautiful,intelligent and talented we are.

We embody, what is have been chosen, given and earned, to pass it to others, to inspire them, to motivate and to make their simple day brighter.

Dont seek to be the new Da Vinci or the second Mozart. There are never "new ones" or "second ones". There is only the one and only. There is only Unique. And YOU are unique. And Life/Universe needs exactly YOUR talents and gifts. Needs them NOW. Because You were given them for this particular life time and they match perfectly exactly this time/space sequence.

Throughout this book we talk about an importance of moving forward. As far as Life/Universe is constantly moving forward, expanding and evolving.

Here is the same. Talents and gift You hold inside You are talents and gifts that are not supposed to be opened and expressed in the eternal "tomorrow". You hold them to share them NOW.

You can,obviously, work on Your creative ideas and master Your art skills,but to make a first step towards expressing Your creativity is vitally important. Start with the small steps,but START.

We all have busy schedules and many things to do,but dont let this home/work routine to dull Your Divine sprakle. Because its not only "Yours", its rather "through You".

See Yourself as a channel from the Divine down to Earth. Because thats exactly who You truly are .

Life/Universe already has Da Vinci and Mozart, Tolstoy and Shakespeare and many, many others. Those are geniouses, who´s talent shines for eternity. But...

Thats not enough .

YOU, YOUR talent, YOUR gift, YOUR key is a part of Life/Universe as well and as far as You are here,on Earth, thats exactly what Life/Universe needs – YOU. YOUR way, YOUR style, YOUR expression of Yourself, YOUR authenticity. Exactly how YOU do it.

This book,for instance, would have never been written, if I would continue to "hide" what i have to share. You, me and many of us was told ¨to be modest¨¨¨ and to listen what other, ¨¨¨intelligent¨, ¨wise¨, ¨old¨ people say.

Its OK and sometimes very right to listen to other people, when those ¨others¨ are really wise ones, but if You also have something to say, to show, to sing, to draw, to dance, to créate – DO IT. Its given to You,its given THROUGH You, its here – to share.

This book would have never seen a day light, if I would continue to procrastinate the expression of myself and keep on thinking, that ¨many books are already written and why even give it a try¨.

But one day i just realised,that i have what i have exactly in the way it shoul be. In the way Life/Universe wants me to share it and that there are people who need it exactly THIS way.

And those people, in turn, have what I need. And in this order we grow together and enrich each other and therefore – enrich the Life itself. The Universe itself.

Dont let modesty, shyness, doubts and nay-sayers around You to fetter Your talent and to bury Your gifts.

Life/Universe needs what exactly YOU have to propose and to share. Dont look at the others and dont compare Yourself with anyone else (if i would compare myself with Louise Hay, i would never have a courage to write a single word).

YOU and YOUR talents and YOUR gifts are unique and the way YOU express them (and therefore – Yourself) – thats what Life/Universe needs. Dont fake things. There is no creativity in fake .

Within You - You have just enough to make it perfect.

Perfect not according to society standarts, but according to YOU.

"War and Peace", "Romeo and Juliet" would never have been written, if Tolstoy and Shakespeare would compare themselves to others and were trying to write like the others.

Dont let "big names" scare You. In the eyes of the Universe we are all equal and loved. And talented. And gifted.

Find, feel Your gift, Your Key - the "stuff" You came here to share with us, to enrich all of us.

We need it .

CHAPTER 8

Time And Discipline.

I want to talk about the importance of being on time.

Yes, we all know,that its not "polite" to come late and too make another person/persons to wait. But is it really only that? Or there is something deeper,than just good manners.

Yes. There is something deeper,than etiquette. There IS something more,than just being polite.

We already know,that Universe is not just a chaos of unorganized events and coincidents (which simply dont exist). Universe is governed by spiritual laws. And Universe has discipline as well. And being "disciplined" by its substance,Universe supports discipline. And as we can see, great results are normally are achieved by people with great self-discipline. And discipline has its timing.

If we dont have a habbit of being on time,we risk to lose many opportunities,which Universe has for us.

Its like with the business meetings.

Imagine You have an appointment with the CEO of Your company and its about a big project,which is considering to be leading by You. And You are constantly being late. We are all human beings (here,on Earth) and indeed,on the way to the office many things can happen. Once. Or maybe twice. But not all the time. Universe/Life is not something intangible or what You cant see or feel or touch. Universe/Life is EVERYTHING. Universe is PEOPLE as well. People who are waiting for You. Making someone waiting for You, You disrespect not only that particular person. Through him or her You disrespect the whole Universe. And like with the example with the CEO,who is waiting for You to discuss Your leadership in the new big project,Universe can (and will) feel ¨tired¨ of Your not showing up on time and will pass the project to another person. Who,probably,is not that talented or professional enough,but who,having self-discipline,comes on time and keeps her/his word,will finally do the job not worse,than You. Or maybe even better.

So in the case with the Universe/life its the same.

I suppose we all know one or two (or more) people around us,who are being not super smart or incredibly talented,but due to their discipline and determination,those people achieved good or even great results in their lives. And we might also know some persons,who being talented and gifted(but without self-discipline and will power) spent their lives if not in misery,but obvioulsy not on the level of their potential.

Not everyone is born with self-discipline and inner knowing/feeling of importance of being on time. But these skills can be learned and mastered. And to achieve in life what You want,these skills must be learned and mastered.

Im talking not only about professional career. Im talking about everything – about spirituality as well. There is no,for example, too much sense to meditate once a month(or once a week). Spiritual work – is WORK. And like any other work it requires time, consistency and determination.

To raise Your spiritual level, You have to build Your spiritual muscles. And one cant build muscles,if one goes to the gym once a month,right?

Life/Universe is never static,it always moves forward. Life/Universe will not wait for You with all the gifts and opportunities forever. If You are not on time at the place where You should be,sooner or later will become a moment,when Universe will not be there for You either.

Be on time.

Respect the Universe,who is waiting for You. Because the person who is waiting for You – IS Universe. It doesn't matter if its Your best friend("We know each other for years! She/he can wait!"), Your employee or a neighbour. Its never about them. Its always about YOU. Show the Universe,that it can count on you. So next time You can count on Universe. Be there and be on time.

People can hold the concept of discipline/time as a life-lesson which they have chosen to learn or to master in this life time. Normally in this case such people have very (sometimes to extremes) organised partners (learning through personal relationship is one of the most effective(and the most emotionally charged) way to learn),so they learn from each other to reach the balance between a total disorganization/chaos and the discipline,which does not let ¨to breath¨ and to enjoy life. Because everything is good,when its balanced. And discipline is not a corset. But its better to have it to ¨shape¨ Your life.

But does to have discipline means constantly to be under the pressure of self-control and feeling like living a life without a chance to breath? No,thats not the case. We are here to be happy,not to suffer under self made restrictions(we have them enough from society). And being spirits,temporaly having a human being form,we need to be attentive to ALL our needs. And these needs also and ultimately include a need for relaxation and rest. And ironically,by taking care about Your physical needs (like having enough time to sleep,to eat good,to have time just for Yourself), You are equally taking care about Your spiritual needs.

Taking rest is NOT a stop. Taking rest,recharging Your batteries… is also moving forward.

Everything is energy. And our ¨task¨ here,on Earth,is to ¨work¨ on our energy to keep it as high and pure as it is posible in our personal/individual conditions. And its not posible to be on the high frequency,when You are constantly tired. There always should be a balance and while in the physical body,we cant deny physical needs. And if Your body is telling You,that instead of deep 2 hours meditation early in the morning, You just need these 2 hours of an extra sleep,then – listen to the wisdom (and the need) of the body and spend these 2 hours sleeping. Universe is constantly using our bodies as the perfect way to communicate with us and to guide us for our highest good.

If in the hot summer vacation day You read another spiritual book out of feeling that You HAVE to read it(not to lose all Your spirituality in 10 days),but not because You want to read it…and what You really actually feel to read, is some love or detective story.. then put Your spiritual book aside and take what You really feel like to read.

Taking a rest is NOT a stop in Your journey. Its actually is an absolute move with the Flow Of Life. Because listening to Your body and taking care about Your needs NOW,when its needed,its living exactly in that Magic Flying NOW,where and when Universe always "lives".

And if instead of listening Your body,the Wisdom of Your body and have an extra sleep, You wake up at 4am out of "obligation" to meditate only because somewhere and thousand(s) years ago monks were meditating at this precise time… well… You are not only neglecting Your physical body needs (and therefore – Your health), You are living in that "somewhere" thousand(s) years ago. You are not in the NOW. And what was perfect and right for someone in some monastery a thousand years ago,has nothing to do with YOU and with YOUR NOW.

Universe/Life is constantly moving forward and all humanity is moving and evolving with it. The secret of living and evolving in that magic Flow Of Life is to listen to Your inner voice,which knows Your unique life plan which does not resemble to any others life plan. And in Your life plan could be easily "written" that at 4am You should sleep,not meditate.

To listen and to follow Your inner voice and guidance is the best way to build and to master Your self-discipline. Because through Your inner voice Your spiritual helpers(guardian angels,spirit guides,etc.) communicate with You All The Time and they always act in Your best interests. If You learn to trust and – not less important! – to FOLLOW Your inner guidance,then You will be always in the ¨discipline¨ of the Universe, always in The Flow Of Life. Because to be in The Flow is ¨to listen¨ The Flow and to follow it.

And believe me,Flow knows,when its Your personal time to work and when its Your personal time to rest.

Dont forcé anything and dont build Your life according to some rules,which were written hundreds/thousands years ago. Lot of things changed from that time. And You are not the person it was written for.

Always listen to Yourself,ALL is in inside You. And this ¨ ALL¨ knows Your perfect timing for work and for everything else.

Dont confuse this inner wisdom/guidance with the ego, though.

Ego might be telling You ¨Why to go to the office?! Its my time to rest! I feel it!¨ But Your inner truth can sound as ¨ Right now,in this period of my life,im working on my discipline lesson through the job in my company. And i get salary which allows me to have good relaxing time during the weekends and/or vacations(If You are stick to the job,which doesnt fullfil any of Your needs – its another case). And to follow this inner wisdom and to go to the office and to accomplish Your duties is nothing else,than showing to the Universe,that You are a disciplined person.

And trust me,Universe will appreciate that. In a beautiful way. :)

CHAPTER 9

Professional Medical Help

I feel that that topic I want to cover in this chapter is one of the most important ones. Its professional medical help.

Spiritually oriented people sometimes think, that its "not spiritual" to use professional medical treatment.

Its not so uncommon to hear, that as far as we are all spirits, so we can be healed by spirit alone. What in some cases can be true, indeed.

But the truth also is, that for every change/healing modality, one has to be emotionally and physically ready.

And if Your energy is not "high"/elevated enough, then You are not at that high/elevated frequency, where You are able to change Your body/health conditions by thought/intention alone.

People who are able (or expierenced) to heal themselves by thought/intention alone are not necessarily highly spiritual people. It can be as Dr. Joe Dispenza says "absolutely normal people doing unnormal things".

So what is their secret? What let them to elevate their energy/frequency till that degree, when healing by thought alone becomes possible?

The key is their focus. Because if they are permanently focused on their main and ultimate goal – health – they elevate their frequency high enough by sending all their energy constantly to the one direction; therefore, they have enough ammount of very high/pure/¨undisturbed¨ energy, which does not resonate with the frequency of the dis´ease anymore and this is where healing by thought/intention alone takes place.

But not every person posesses enough of that intention or will power to make this kind of healing happen.

People tend to be distracted by many things and in many ways and when they are seriously ill, most of the time they are distracted by thoughts, which are not in an alignment with the healing. So Universe constantly gets confusing messages from them.

From the one hand, they have an intention to heal themselves without professional medical intervention and during focused meditation this intention could be (or IS) strong enough to make it happen.

But from the other hand – when they are ¨out¨ of the quantum field (distracted by negative thoughts/images about their health), their thoughts have lower vibrational frequencies, which are not in alignment with the healing by thought/intention alone.

My view is that we always have to be grounded and we should never forget, that Universe ¨works¨ through the people as well. And sometimes these people happen to be professional medics.

In other words, when Your le gis broken, call Angels for help. And call the ambulance right away.

Progress and medical help is a part of the Universe and therefore – exist to serve us, to help us and to heal us as well.

Every kind of medical help exists,because its a part of the Universe and its there for a reason. And this reason, most of the times, is to help us to heal.

There is really no need to separate ¨spiritual healing¨ (meditations,affirmations,etc.) and professional medical. They can (and in my opinión – should) perfectly work together and this combination of science and spirituality can help us to heal (or to improve ourhealth) in a shorter ammount of time, than if we would use them separately.

Universe ¨works¨ through medics and hospitals as well.

I want to make an emphasis here : Universe Works through medics and hospitals as well.

Spirituality and progress are NOT separated. They are a part of our current reality and exist simultaneously. And we have a great privilege (the privilege the humans of our race have never had before) to use benefits from both.

Through the progress Universe expands/expresses itself and if we are going against the progress, we are going against the Flow of Life.

Of course,its important and desirable, in case of western(¨professional¨) medical intervention to have a doctor, who is, if not aware about the underlying causes of the physical manifestations in Your body (dis´eases), but, at least, is not against Your willing to take a holistic/ complete approach to Your treatment.

According to the Law of Attraction, You will "attract" a doctor, who is perfect for You in this particular time and space sequence.

But it also means, that You have to chose carefully and always trust Your inner voice. If after the first appointment with a doctor You dont feel comfortable (and uplifted), then its a sign, that its better for You to search for another one. So here You can ask – but what about The Law of Attraction? If I "attracted" that particular doctor, but dont feel comfortable with her/him, does not that mean, that i should stick to this doctor anyway (according to that i "attracted" her/him) and not to listen to myself, to my inner voice, my gut feeling?

The answer is "no". We should always listen our inner voice. Because no one, except ourselves, does not know/ feel better our life plan. And here,according to Your life plan and Your life lessons, might be Your lesson to say "NO" to this particular doctor /clinic/treatment and/or to trust Yourself, Your inner voice and the doctor was drawn to You "to teach" You exactly this lesson.

Its also possible,that that particular doctor needed YOU and Your spiritual approach to healing to start to open him/herself up to that direction.

It does not mean,that You have to continue "to teach" that person (the doctor in this case) her/his lesson on and on – Your part/role can be very Little and short – but that definitely means,that You have to be honest with Yourself. And if You dont feel comfortable in the presence of Your doctor, its reasonable to start to search for another one.

Everything is energy.

And energy is Your life forcé. The life forcé You always

need. Especially when Your body temporaly lives in the health limiting conditions. So if You under the treatment of the doctor You dont feel comfortable with, it means, that every time,when You even think about Your doctor, Your energy level – You life forcé – is going down.

So basically the more often You see Your doctor You dont feel comfortable with,the more energy will be drained from You. Physically (and likely temporally) You could start feel better at some point and to some degree, but if after the appontiment You feel tired emotionally or even exhausted, Your healing process will never go with the same speed and results,as if You were ¨in the team¨ with a specialist, whose frequency/energy would be in the perfect match with Yours; who,for example, would be sharing Your holistic approach to Your treatment. In this case great results could be achieved.

Professional medical help ¨mixed¨ with positive affirmations and meditations is a tremendously powerful cocktail against any dis´ease.

A friend of mine who had digestión problems took holistic approach to her treatment and achieved good results combining professional medical help and meditations.

The first doctor she had an appointment with, did not find anything, even though to that moment,my friend already had couple of months of digestive problems. She was already doing healing meditations,but the situation did not improve. So she found another specialist, who, after numerous tests, finally diagnosed a gastrit. Together they elaborated her treatment plan, which included taking medicines and a special diet. She also was doing her meditations and had a trust that everything is going well and to the right direction. And this combined spiritual and medical work gave a wonderful result.

Dont be a ¨black and white¨ - person, because the world is not black and white.

If You accept and enjoy benefits from the progress (using professional western medical help,for example), that does not mean, that You ¨betray¨ spirituality.

In fact, it means that You accept Life/Unniverse in all its variety and all the gifts in it. And THAT is authentic spirituality.

Being spiritual does not mean to come back to the caves and huts. Being spiritual means to enjoy Life and always move forward.

And we can not move forward, if we dont feel well and deny help, that progress offers to us.

If one suddenly has a severe headache and for example, has to participate in an important event or meeting, its reasonable to take a pill and to perform one's best, than not to take it and not to do Your best in the important moment (not only for Your,but for another people as well).

Me,personally, im trying to avoid pills the máximum I can,but in some circumstances a sudden strong headache, can interfere important plans and in this case i take a pill and after, when a moment come, i definitely take a rest,because through pain or uncomfortable feelings my body gave me a sign to do so.

Its important to be grounded and reasonable. Medicines are also part of the Universe and exist for a reason. Dont abuse Your body with them (chemicals are still chemicals), but neither deny them only because its not ¨spiritual¨. We are here not to suffer and to be in pain.

We are here to be happy. Healthy and happy. :)

CHAPTER 10

Words

We (or many of us) used to think,that actions ¨speak¨ louder,than words and there is a big truth in that, indeed. But i would like to make You reflect on the following concept :

¨Trust words. Listen ¨through¨ the words and trust what You hear¨. What is meant by that?

A good old truth - everything is energy. And every word has its frequency. Its very easy to understand and to feel by simply saying(or mentally saying) two different words. Love and hate,for example. Grief and joy. Fear and freedom. And so forth. By saying out loud(or mentally) these words,note Your feelings. Im more than sure,that the feelings You will feel by pronouncing,for example, ¨joy¨ would be completely different from what You will feel by saying ¨grief¨. Because,as discussed above,everything has its own vibrational match.

"Heavy" words have heavy energy. "Light",beautiful words have high,light energy.

Didn't You notice,that if You are around people who swear a lot,You dont feel comfortable? Because swearing words have low, "heavy" energy and being sensitive and being sensitive to these vibrations (and as far as You are reading this book, You likely are), Your energy field (aura) is being sort of under the attack of the low energy arrows. And people, who use swear words a lot.. are not happy with their life and themselves people.

Thats why in the beginning of this chapter i proposed You to trust the words and to listen "through" them. A person can laugh and smile,but if his/her language is not "clean",then there is "something". Our natural state,as being a part of the pure light,is high and pure energy. Joy and contentment with life is our natural state. Because we, all of us, are beloved children of the Universe. And if we constantly low our energy level (through using swear words in this particular case),it means,that there is some trigger inside us,that makes us to do it. And the more we swear,the more lower energy/people/circumstances/life situations we attract into out lives.

Because what we give,that we receive and we attract what we ARE(NOT what we want).

I give You an example with my neighbour,who desperatley wanted to find a new appartement to rent to move in. He was searching for about 2 years(what is quite a big time for the big city where we live in),but without any successful result. And for me it was very clear why he could not get,what he wanted. Being born and raised in a very emotional country, he always expressed himself till extremes and used such an ammount of swear words,that it was difficult for me to be a long time next to him(and i never was). So the way he was talking about the real estate agencies and/or the owners of the flats he was seeing,was always very negative and he described his expierences with them with a massive "help" of swear words.

What we give,that we receive.

Obviously he was constantly "giving" low energy into the Field and Universe just had no any chance "to praise" him with what he desired the most - a good new appartment. The messages he was constantly sending to the Universe were all about,that all real estate agent are as...les and the owners of the appartments are not better and all of them are just using the situation on the market to earn more money.

What we give,that we receive.

So during 2 years,when i was ocasionally crossing with him on the street,i was constantly listening the same swear words and the same complains. Once i tried to give him a very slight idea about the importance of changing his lexic (and therefore – and ultimatley – thoughts and from here – energy) about this situation,if he really wants it to be changed in a better for him way,but it seems he was not ready for this kind of information. I dont know if he finally found another place to live,but this situation showed me – again – the importance of watching our language.

Watch,observe the words You are using. They are indicators of the frequency You are in. By changing Your words, You will change Your frequency and therefore – Your life.

Easy to say and well...not so easy to do.

If You are raised in the environment,where using swear words was something natural,then the habit of using them on a constant basis is likely has strong roots in You. But no panic. Everything is posible. And every single step is a victory. Dont be sad or angry at Yourself,that after making a decisión to watch Your words and to eliminate (or reduce) the presence of swear words in Your daily language You still use them. One step at a time.

If 30 (or more. or less) years You were very comfortable with Your lexic (but maybe not with Your life. And everything is connected),its likely,that You will not change this situation in one single day. Be patient and kind to Yourself. If instead,lets say,10 "bad" words today You said 9 – its already a step to the brighter future and new,more "pure" life.

Of course,that should not work as an excuse for You,that after a year of "trying" You are still saying daily those 9 words instead of 10,motivating Yourself,that "its already a big achievement"(for a day – yes,for a year -no). Be patient with Yourself,but feel the limit where Your patience transforms in stagnation and You dont move further anymore. This is the moment,when You have to become "serious" with Yourself and give Yourself a little (or a big) push (if You really want changes,of course).

Always keep in mind, that everything is energy and information. If You are willing to change Your life and/ or to become a better versión of Yourself, You have to work in Your WHOLE energy field. It means,that only affirmations,only meditations and/or only "positive" thoughts – its just a part of a larger picture. And this larger picture consists of Your language as well. More than that - what and how You say is a BIG part of Your energy field. Because being a human, You likely communicate a lot. So if Your lexic vibrates on the low frequency, YOU are on the low frequency and You are constantly sending confusing messages to the Universe. From the one hand – You are using affirmations,prayers etc.(high energy),but from the other hand – on Your daily basis Your energy is still low and doesn´t let desirable changes to happen.

Because affirmations and prayers is something, what has ¨limited time¨,but the way You coomunicate throughout the day – is almost limitless. So guess ¨who¨ wins.

Its All is One and everything is connected. So yes,Your language,the words You are saying and using influence Your whole life and more than that – the life of the people around You as well. Your energy is not separated from anyone else and we all have an impact one to another.

So if one uses swear words,he/she lowers not only his/her energy level,but also an energy level of the people around.

I guess, we all had a chance in our lives to realise,that its ¨heavy¨ to be around the people, who´s language is far away from that one we can call ¨respectful¨ towards the others.

Me,personally,for myself i made a commitment long time ago – i care about myself and i care about my energy(and i care about the people and energy around me). So i watch my words,my language and if i say something,what is not ¨clean¨ by its energy thats normally very rare case(and yes,no one is saint). And even though i was raised in the environment where swear words were very,very rare to hear and i never used it on a daily basis,but still. There always can be a situation, when You are out of balance and control and You can suddenly express Yourself through the "dirty" language. Don't blame Yourself if it happened,but also dont let "Im just a human after all" be Your permanent excuse. Yes, You (we all are) are a human being with all Your weak and strong sides,but always remember,that we are here to work on ourselves and to make ourselves (and therefore – the world) better; not to be the same persons we were 5,10,20 etc.years ago. And if You really want to change Your reality for the better one, You have to work on ALL aspects of Your life. And "clean",pleasant language You speak,is one of these aspects.

And dont be shy or afraid to gently point Your Friends and/or Your family members, if they swear to much and You dont feel comfortable with that. But always do it with love and respect.

We are not here to work on others. We are here to work on ourselves,but that doesn't mean,that we have quetly handle everything whats going on around us and keep our mouth shut,if our friends/ loved ones dont respect our need to communicate proprely.

Try to explain Your circle,that You value a lot "clean" language and thank them to make this "effort" for You(but the truth is also is,that they are doing it for themselves as well;)

If people,whom You call "friends" or "loved ones" dont pay attention to Your need and ignore Your request,then its time to ask Yourself a question,if these people really has right to be called Your ¨friends¨ and/or ¨loved ones¨.

Everything is energy and once You start to work on Your energy(without working on someone else), You will see,that people around You start to change as well.

What kind of chnages that will be? There are two options : or people around You will also start to pay attention on how and what they say and start to change themselves (and therefore- their lives and therefore – the world) for the better versión of themselves. Or... step by step these people will leave Your life to free the space for those ones,who will be on the same frequency – the new,higher frequency You hold now. And dont be afraid of that change. Embrace it. Because when You work on Yourself and become a new, better versión of You,everything what comes into Your life is also always better.

Law of attraction.

CHAPTER 11

Dreams

Spiritually oriented people normally seek for deep interpretations of dreams.

And indeed, some dreams - being a gateaway to the ¨unknown¨/other dimensions – carry an important and useful information within.

There are many dream-guides, which are designed to help us to understand the meanings of our dreams. The one i use, for example,is Denise Linn's ¨The Hidden Power of Your dreams¨.

When i have a dream, which has clear images and/or details (such as,for example,mountains,animals,objects,colours etc.), the interpretation from this guide-book is normally very accurate.

I say ¨normally¨,because sometimes there is no a deep hidden meaning in our dreams and what we see in the night and remember in the morning – is just the reflections of our subconscious mind.

These dreams are not "prophetic" and no need to waste time in searching something, what doesnt exist.

Spiritual people have tendency to look for a deep meaning in everything and sometimes they become ungrounded in interpretations of their dreams and start to seek "the truth" or guidance, when our mind just wonders during the night.

When i stepped on my spiritual path and the path of self – discovery,i was also trying to find a deep meaning in every dream i saw.

Indeed, most of the times i was (and still i am:) quite accurate in interpretations and understanding my dreams and they were reflections of the reality and events, i was expierencing in the dream, i was actually expierencing and/or was supposed to expierence in my reality.

But there were also times, when my dreams were just my minds inner journeys, which were not holding deep meanings. It was more likely sort of feeling of thoughts passing by.

Human mind is curious and powerful mechanism and if needed, its capable to find (or rather – to build) a hidden meaning in everything.

My key point in here is that sometimes a dream is just a thought – form floating by and there is no need to stress Yourself in trying to interpretate it. Just acknowledge its existence and let it go.

Its posible, that later You will find the meaning of that dream, but its also posible,that not. I have a couple of dreams, which i remember pretty clear, but i still, after few years, didnt figure out, what they were trying "to tell" me. I let it go.

Dreams under the state of the intoxication. Dreams with a "foreign" energy involved.

The topic i want to discuss now is not widely covered and i see it important to bring some light on it. I see it useful to talk about alien energy/entities, which some people hold in their energy field.

These entities can project their vibrations/"thoughts" in our dreams and we can take them for our owns.

Most frequently we can be influenced by earthbounded spirits, especially when person is deeply emotionally attached to someone; who passed away and cant/doesn't want "to move" forward.

If, lets say, a mother of her passed away son can't and/or doesn't want to let him go and becomes very attached to his energy, she constantly feeds him with with her energy and makes his attachment to Earth even stronger. And not only attachment itself. Being constanly fed by her energy, his energy becomes strong enough to interfere her thoughts and moods.

The spirit, who in the physical realm for was her son, also becomes able to manifest himself or his thought-forms in her dreams. And in this case mothers dreams are literally her "sons" "dreams".

Thats why, for instance, parents who are not capable tovlet their passed away children go, see them so often in their dreams (and not necessary, that these dreams are "good" ones).

Being attached to Earth, some spirits can get "bored" and in order to get an "attention"(boost of energy from ther spirits in physical form(humans), they could intertain themselves by interfering in the dream-states of the others.

In this case there is really no need to look for a sense in the dream, but whats necessary to do is to check one's energy field on the subject "is it "my" dream"? If Your intuition/inner voice is telling You, that may be, what You have seen at night is not "Yours", then its time to ask Yourself a question "Who is it in my energy field"?

The same is about our moods and moods swings. Highly sensitive people and empaths (its not the same), who are not protected enough from low energy, can expierence mood swings without any seeming reasons.

It can also be a "fault"of an "alien" energy in our energy field.

If we spend time in crowded places (bars,stadiums,etc.), there is a hight risk "to catch" and to be influenced by "alien" energy. Thats why, for instance,so many normally pacific people start arguments and/or fights in bars, discos, etc. Being influenced by "foreign" energies, they literally become someone else for a period of time and can behave or say things, which are not common for their "normal" behaviour. In movies we get used to see it as "voices in the head", which can also take this form. But most of the time, it is, lets say, quite, silent "invasion".

Me, personally, if i find myself in a "weird" mood and there is no any particular reason for that, i check myself if this mood is really "mine".

How "to check" it?

Just sit quietly and with a calm mind and quite state and ask Yourself - "If this mood is really mine? ". Stay still and listen quietly Your inner voice. The answer will and can come in different forms – a thought, an image or a feeling. Trust Yourself and You will be guided. In most of the cases You will feel if the energy is Yours or not and if its not, make a gentle propose to that energy/entity to go to the Light or to any other place, where the energy/entity may feel comfortable and safe.

The reason why its necessary to give that energy an option where to go (to the Light or to the safe place), is that some spirits (energy/entity) dont feel comfortable with the idea of going to the Light. Some of them are afraid of being ¨punished¨ - cases, when the spirit is aware of his/her ¨unproper¨ behaviour in previous physical form or spirits, who in the last ¨human life¨ were raised under the pressure of strong religious traditions, where being a ¨sinner¨ and ¨going to hell¨ were dominant concepts. And in some cases earthbounded spirits can also assosiate Light with harm, pain and danger – in cases of the death in fire, for example.

Normally after checking Your energy field on the subject of the presence an ¨alien¨ energy and asking/proposing that energy to leave, the spirit leaves.

(If not, thats the case of checking the reasons, why the spirit is attached to You/the place/the object and asking for professional help).

Mood swings are common after visiting crowded places – such as stadiums, bars, big shopping malls etc. In other words, where there is a lot of different (due the presence of different people) energy is accumulated and earthbounded spirits can ¨feed¨ themselves from this common ¨feeder¨.

If You are highly sensitive and Your energy field is not

strong enough, there is a risk, that someone will "stick" to You and You will come back in a company You didnt ask for.

So how to protect Yourself from an uninvited guests?

Ask Archangel Michael to put his blue cloak of protection around You and/or set an intention (in case You are not familiar with angelic realms), that nothing,what is not from the Light, can go through it. After visiting crowded places(concerts,sports events etc.) wash Your clothes You were in without waiting. Everything is energy and even if You came home realivetly clear, still You "brought" some energy with You. To be completely in YOUR energy field, You need to have máximum YOUR energy around. So yes, after parties, big events or simply being in a company, which is not "Yours", wash Your clothes withiut waiting.

The same goes about the dreams. If before going to sleep energywise You dont feel comfortable, always ask archengel Michael to protect You. If You are not familiar with Archangels energy, ask directly God/Universe/Life/Jesus/whatever feels closer to You to protect You from anything, what is not from the Light.

DREAMS IN A TOXIC STATE.

When people go to sleep in a toxic state (under alcohol or any type of drugs), they often see "weird" dreams. And there is no sense to search for a meaning in that night (or day) journeys. When we abuse our bodies with alcohol and/or drugs, our energy field becomes very weak and easy to the "foreign" energy to enter and therefore – to influence us. And at the same time, when we are in this toxic state, our frequency is too low to allow our spiritual helpers to help and to protect us fully. So we are becoming very vulnerable to the astral entities and low energy vibrations.

Thats why, for instance, the house can be full with any kind of religious icons, images and statues, but if the persons who inhabit the place, abuse their bodies with toxic substances, they dont feel nor happy nor protected. And its not ¨God´s fault¨. They, themselves, are lowering their frequencies to that state, where the help, protection and support from the Light is hardly achievable. The power is never in the ¨object¨.

The power is always in YOU.

CHAPTER 12

We Are Always Doing Our Best

Yes.

We are always doing our best. We and all the other people around us.

Sometimes its difficult to see and to admit it, but the truth is, that everything we are doing (or not doing), we are doing (or not doing) in order to make ourselves to feel better.

We used to blame ourselves and the others with frases like ¨You could do better¨. But there is a difference between ¨ You could do better¨ and ¨ You can do better¨.

¨ You could do better¨ can hold the frequency of blame, regreat and reproach, while ¨You can do better¨ can sound as an uplifting and motivational push.

In the most cases ¨You could do better¨ doesn´t serve our highest good, because we tend to spend too much time in the past and keep on regret what could have been done ¨better¨(or in a different way).

Yes,there are always ways to do it ¨better¨, but You/we/they did it the way You/we/they did and at that point of time it was really Your/our/their best.

We were raised in the culture, where we have been taught constantly to compare ourselves with the others. First it likely was in the kindergarden, then probably with the children of the neighbours, later with the schoolmates, then in the university and at work and...here we go! We compare ourselves with the others our entire life!

Some of us are completely unaware and the others simply forget, that each and every one of us has her/his unique life purpose, individual life plan and personal life path.

Yes, we are all unlimited and powerful beings and with enough constant focus on the desirable goal we can achieve things, which could be considered ¨impossible¨ regarding our body/health/age conditions, but the question is... Is to do something equally good or ¨better¨, than our neighbour/schoolmate/collegue does, is really better for us?

Let me give You an example. Lets take a profesional high level sportsman with perfect physical conditions, who's life is sport and competitions.

Im fond of sport and im doing sport all my life. Not on the professional level. Just for pleasure.

Yes,sometimes there are the days, when im a bit lazy and i think, that i can skip training and in this case a live example of some professional sportman, who's achievements i admire, serves me as a good motivational push and i put my snickers on and go to the gym or to train outside. And i feel great afterwards.

But there are also days,when i feel tired and my only mood is to relax on the sofá with a good book. And in this case I dont put my snickers on, i dont go to the gym and… i feel great afterwards.

Because being a professional high level sportman is NOT MY life path. Its NOT me. And i dont need to train in the gym every day to achieve my goals, because our goals – the goal of the professional sportman and mine – are different ones and the ways to achieve them are different as well. This book would not be written if i were spending all the time in the gym. And many Olimpic medals would not be won if their owners instead of trainings and preparing for competitions would be writing books.

Indeed, in some moments of my ¨lazyness¨ an example of someone, who achieved great results in her/his sport career can motivate me not to skip training and to do some fitness instead of staying on the sofá and i always keep in mind, that ¨ You can have results or excuses. Not both¨(Arnold Schwarzenegger) and i put my snickers on and i go to the gym(or outside) and i feel just great after – because of my little victory over myself.

But in the case of taking necessary self-care, its ultimately important to listen to YOURSELF, not to look, what and how others are doing and living, no matter how much sometimes those ¨others¨ can motivate You in the other day. Because it is YOU and only YOU, who knows, whats better for YOU and for YOUR life. So….

Staying at home on the sofá, for a professional sportman during the time of preparing for competitions, would not the best option. But for ME, according to MY needs, MY circumstances and and MY life, staying at home on the sofá, when i feel a need for that – its really the best option.

So if i were a professional sportman and would go to the gym, when i dont feel like – i would have done my best. But being ME and not going to the gym having ¨i need just to relax¨- mood – i would also have done my best.

We should always keep in mind, that we all have different life plans and we are doing our best indeed in following those plans.

Its good to motivate and to cheer other people up, but NEVER push anybody to do something. You can direct, guide and give a kind and honest opinon and/or advice. But never push. You dont know the life plan of the other person and whats ¨better¨ for You could be completely out of the other persons life plan and therefore – not for the highest good of anyone. A person could be simply not ready (for many reasons,inlcuding karmic patterns) for a ¨better¨ life/job/friendships/relationships and thats why he/she is really doing his/her best according to his/her ¨level¨.

Every decisión we make or dont make goes out of the desire to feel better and we are doing our best to reach this ¨feeling better¨. So there is never a need to regret about the past and blame oneself and/or the others for not doing our/their best.

According to our life plans and time/space circumstances we always do our best.

Its easy ¨to fall¨ from this position and to come back to the ¨good old down to earth¨ model of thinking and start to regret and to reflect on ¨what could have been done¨ and/or ¨what could have been done better¨, but always keep in mind, that everything is energy and has its own frequency and according to that particular situation/circumstances(according to that frequency), we were doing our best due our desire/need to feel better.

I highly recommend Robert Schwarz¨s books and his profound researches on the pre-birth planning and following our life-plans. His work demonstartes brilliantly, that even if here, on Earth, we consider some our life events or actions as ¨huge mistakes¨, but from the higher perspective its always just a small part of the larger picture and serves our higher purpose and therefore – the higher purpose of all the Universe.

Stagnation and doing nothing should never be an ¨im just doing my best accoring to my life plan¨ - excuse, but listening Your inner voice (even if it tells to stop and literally do nothing) and following it – its always ¨doing Your best¨.

Dont compare ¨Your best¨ with someone else´s ¨best¨. There is no sense in that. We are all unique and one of a kind. But again – to have a role model, who´s achievements motivate You, is not a bad thing either at all.

Always ask Yourself, why are You trying to do it as or ¨better¨, than X does it? Is it because X really motivates You to move forward and on X-example You see, that there is really no limits or because You just want to prove to Your parents/friends/neighbours, how ¨cool¨ You are and that You are ¨worthy¨? If its the first respond – keep on going, You are doing it for YOURSELF and therefore – its for Your highest good. If its a respond number 2 – slow down. Option number 2 is an ¨ego-option¨.

And its time to ask Yourself "Why are You doing, what You are doing and for whom really You are doing it"? If You are not doing it for Yourself, You will never achieve Your real "best". Because the outer reason of Your work can disappear one day (parents can die and partner can leave) and You will lose all Your motivation and probably (and likely) You will realise, how much time and energy went to the wrong direction.

Always monitor the underlying intention of Your work/actions. You will really do Your best, if You will do it to make YOURSELF a better version of You, not when You try to impress someone or to prove something to somebody.

Always keep in mind – You literally do Your best, because there is nobody In The Whole Universe, who can do it exactly YOUR way. And Universe needs YOUR way, because Universe expands through YOU as well.

So do YOUR best. And do it YOUR way.

Afterword

For Gennady Zelenov. With Love and Gratitude. This book would have never been written without him and conditions he provided for this work.

And for All of Us.

Life is Magic.